THE ADVENTURES OF LAMBKIN THE CAT

The Adventures of Lambkin the Cat

JILL KELLEY WIDMANN

Charleston, SC
www.PalmettoPublishing.com

The Adventures of Lambkin the Cat
Copyright © 2021 by Jill Kelley Widmann

First Edition

Hardback ISBN: 978-1-64990-662-5
Paperback ISBN: 978-1-64990-664-9

ILLUSTRATIONS BY KRISTI PARNHAM

LAMBKIN WORD SEARCH BY GIA BRAINERD

This book is dedicated to my beloved mother, who taught me to always be compassionate and kind; my beloved father, who taught me about courage and conviction; my dear sister Wendy Jo, who supports and encourages me in all things; my angel Kitty Boo; my angel Pony Baja; all of the animals in the world; and of course, my sweet Lambkin.

SPECIAL THANKS

Special thanks to Kristi Parnham, Jennifer von Geldern, Allie Claire, Corrine Jang Hernandez, Lana Phillips, Deborah Nicol, Gia Brainerd, and Dr. Billie Martin and staff at The Cat Hospital for their support and contributions.

TABLE OF CONTENTS

Preface

Follow the adventures of Lambkin, a clever kitty who occasionally needs help from her friends. Children and adults alike will fall in love with Lambkin's winsome wit, her kitty capers, and her feminine feline sensibilities, and they will learn the importance of respecting animals large and small.

Lambkin knows right from wrong, but sometimes she needs insight from her circle of friends—from her big sister Boo, her Mama Jill, Tino the Mouse, Baja the Pony, and Lady Bug Beetle. She will seek their guidance, and all the pals she meets along the way will make sure she stays safe and makes good choices.

Throughout Lambkin's tales, children will encounter some of life's simple temptations and discover greater meaning behind some actions that may seem harmless. Along with Lambkin, they will learn that their choices affect a great many things—for better or for worse.

Based on the story of a real-life rescue kitty, these simple yet compelling stories will charm you. Real-life photos also add to the effect and magic of Lambkin's adventures. This is what awaits readers of all ages. As Lambkin would say, "Why not give it a try?"

Introduction

Hello, I'm Lambkin, and I am a fuzzy and silly little kitty. You can call me Lambie if you like. I hope that you will accept me as your friend and read all about me and my adventures. I have a lot to say, and there is always something new that I need to talk about.

My favorite color is pink, and I like to eat whenever possible. I am a girl kitty, and sometimes I get into mischief, but I am learning to listen to my mama, as she always knows what is best for me. I always have so much to do, like directing things, playing, being a detective, taking kitty naps, and of course eating. Please tell all of your friends about me and follow me whenever you need to see my fuzzy little face.

Mama says that I am very cute and that I should always spread love. So that is what I am going to do. I am going to spread love and happiness, silliness, and fuzziness.

Let's be buddies!

CHAPTER ONE

Little Lost Lambkin

The Sunflower Drive-In Café is a favorite place for many people in the area surrounding Sacramento. The café is part of the beauty of the quaint little town of Fair Oaks, with its outdoor benches and so many delicious items to eat. A beautiful young kitten, full of life and love, found all sorts of fun as she explored the café in this little village. Unfortunately, the kitten was also lost, but she didn't realize it yet. She was still thrilled at being out in the big, wide world, as there was so much to see and so many bright colors everywhere.

The grass felt good under the kitten's paws, and she loved the way that it smelled. There was still some dew on the grass that made her paws wet. The bright sun seemed to be smiling down on the little town that day. The sky was so pretty and blue, and there were big puffy clouds that looked so soft that the kitten wanted to jump right into them. They were much too high up for that, of course, so the little kitten decided to check out the big sunflowers everywhere. Some of them were bigger than she was! They seemed to smile at her and say, "Hello, little kitten." That is when she started to play games with the sunflowers and run all around them. "This is so much fun!" she exclaimed out loud. The warm sun seemed to get brighter and brighter, and she could hear the sound of people going about their business.

She heard birds singing and other animals busying themselves with their activities as she sniffed, meowed, and ran around on the fresh green grass.

"Look at that! What do I smell? Hey, what's this?" she thought as she frolicked through the bushes and around the tables at the café. How did she get to the café? She wasn't sure—she thought only of what was happening to her *now*. Now was full of fun and adventure, but… what was that feeling in her tummy? Her tummy was making funny noises. "Wait! What is that?" A large white hen, doing her slow chicken walk, was pecking around under the bushes for tidbits to eat. Step, peck, step, peck, peck… The kitten forgot the growing discomfort in her tummy and bounded toward the hen!

"Cluck! Cluck! Cluck!" The hen, catching a glimpse of the running kitten, began to run too. Her toenails went "click, click, click" as she bolted across the Sunflower Drive-In's parking lot with the kitten scrambling along behind.

"Wait! Don't go!" the kitten meowed. "Who are you? Do you want to play?"

As the chicken disappeared into the bushes, the kitten gave up the chase and plunked her little self down on the grass. Suddenly she felt as though something was just not right. "Maybe I am *lost!*" she thought. A man at the café yelled, "Look at the little *lost* kitten!" as he pointed at her. Lost was a word she had heard before, and she understood that it meant that she didn't know where she was or where to go.

Cars made loud noises as they drove by and honked their horns...honk, honk, honk. People talked and laughed, and the kitten started to become scared, as she felt all alone. Her eyes filled with tears.

By this time, the sun was getting dimmer, and the kitten was getting more confused.

"What should I do? Meow, meow. Do I have a mama? What about a family? I don't like being all alone after all…and my tummy feels so funny." She hid her face in her paws and started to cry. Tears streamed down the fur on her little kitten cheeks, and teardrops fell into the blades of grass beneath her.

CHAPTER TWO

The Sunflower Drive-In

Jill and Allie, two good friends, were just pulling into the Sunflower Drive-In Café for a bite to eat when Allie asked, "Did you see that cat chasing that chicken?"

Jill, pulling into a parking spot, answered, "No, but I saw a flash of white!"

That had been the hen—the hen who was long gone. The kitten was not in sight either.

She was hiding under a bush at the sound of the car's big motor. From the bush, she ran to a flowerpot. She peeked out from behind it, secretly watching the girls eating their lunch. After the two young ladies finished their meal and were visiting at their table in the fresh air and sunshine, something amazing happened! The kitten, somehow knowing no human had ever hurt her in her young life, thought, "Why not give it a try?" and bounced up into Jill's lap! One…big…jump…and there she was, sitting there with Jill looking at her in amazement.

Jill still had some crumbs left on her plate, and the kitty quickly gobbled up the remaining bits. "Oh! A kitty just jumped on my lap!" Jill exclaimed, quite astonished, yet delighted. "This kitty is so beautiful with her big blue-gray eyes and her cute little pink nose and mouth. Look, she is so friendly." She took another look and noticed the kitten's fur was a bit grubby, and that she needed some healthy kitten food, as she was quite thin. "I'll bet her coat would be white and fluffy if she were clean! She is such a sweet little kitten. She seems so scared and sad. She must be lost."

The kitten just looked up at Jill with her big eyes as if to say, "Help me, please. I am just a little kitty, and I am lost."

There were still some tears left on her little face, and Jill wiped them off. "You poor little kitten."

As Jill cuddled her, the kitten purred for all to hear: "Purr, Purr, Purr." *Oh, I like her,* thought the kitten. *She smells so nice, and her voice is soft too. I must be a special kitten, because she seems to like me too.*

Time seemed to stand still for a moment. Jill and the little kitten felt so peaceful as Jill continued to hug the fuzzy bundle. The kitten loved being hugged, and felt so warm and cozy as Jill told her that she was going to need a nice bath. People started to gather around, curious to see what was going on. *What a beautiful day this is turning into, and how lucky I am,* thought Jill. The funny thing was, the little kitten was thinking the same exact thing. Birds sang a song of joy, as happiness seemed to glow all around them.

Realizing it was getting late, Jill checked with the people in the café to see if they knew the kitten or where she belonged, but nobody did. One lady said, "The little kitten doesn't seem to have a home or a family." Thinking of the kitten's soiled coat and underfed tummy, Jill asked the girl at the café for an empty box. Carefully putting the kitten in the box and keeping the top open, Jill and Allie drove the little kitten to the veterinarian (animal doctor) at a place called The Cat Hospital.

The ride seemed long to the kitty as she tilted her head every which way to see out of the windows. Cars sped by, but Jill made sure to drive safely and slowly. This was a very important ride and a very important new passenger was with the girls.

When they got to the hospital, the kitten started to become nervous. The hospital was different than anything she had seen before. Going into the building, Jill held the kitten tight, and kept the kitten on her lap when they found a seat. This is when the fuzzy bundle of fur knew that everything was going to be OK. More happiness was in store as the adventure continued.

CHAPTER 3

The Cat Hospital

There were all sorts of cats at The Cat Hospital with all different color combinations of fur. They pushed their faces against the doors of their cat carriers in order to try to get a peek at the newcomer. The kitten could see the little kitty faces and cute little kitty noses peeking through.

Some of the cats meowed loudly, and others were very quiet. The newcomer felt as though all the people and cats at the hospital were there just to greet *her*! This made her feel very special and proud as she sat up straighter to make sure she was noticed by every single person and cat. Jill held on tight enough to let the kitten know that she was not alone.

When it was the kitten's turn to go into one of the rooms, Jill whispered to her, "Everything will be fine, little one. I am right here with you. Don't be frightened, I won't leave you."

Dr. Irene checked the kitten over and gave her a few treatments that all young cats should have. The staff at the hospital were all so great, and the kitten was relieved to find that Dr. Irene was kind and gentle. Dr. Irene assured her that everything would be okay, and this was when the kitten let out a big sigh of relief, as she felt more relaxed now. Doctor Martin and all of the staff, including Sandy, Kristin, Laura, Brandy, Heather, Michele, and Bethany, also agreed that the little kitten was very adorable and sweet and she was lucky that someone who cared about animals had found her.

Dr. Irene checked to see if the kitten had a microchip. A microchip, which is placed at a pet's neck underneath the skin, gives information about the owner in case a pet is ever lost. It is very tiny and doesn't hurt at all. If someone were to find a lost pet and take him or her to an animal hospital, the veterinarian could then tell who the pet belonged to or if the pet had no family.

"This kitten has no chip, Jill," said Dr. Irene as she patted the kitten on the head. "She needs a good home."

Jill knew it was the right thing to do to be the one to give her that home. But Jill still had many worries. What would happen to the kitten if she *didn't* take her home? Would she be fed? Would she be warm? Would she be safe? Those thoughts scared Jill, because she already loved the kitten, and she knew that humans should try to help all animals in need. Helping others is one of the most important things anyone can do, and animals need so much help in this great big world.

Jill couldn't even imagine *not* keeping this little kitty. *I would feel so sad*, she thought. In her heart, she had already made a commitment to the kitten. Jill told the doctor that she would be keeping the little furry one. The doctor then put a microchip with Jill's information under the kitty's skin so that if she ever got lost, the microchip would lead a doctor to contact Jill.

Next, Jill picked out a blue collar with a gold heart that also had important information about the kitten on it. The kitten seemed to know that having a collar was something special, as she leaned forward so Jill could put it on. With the new collar and the new microchip, Jill knew that the kitten would always be safe. Wrapping her up in a pink blanket that one of the staff gave her, Jill said, "You are my sweet kitty, and I will love you always."

With that, she gave the kitten a kiss on the top of her fuzzy head. "I am your mama now. It is time to go to your new home, little one."

CHAPTER 4

Meeting Boo

Leaving the vet, Jill took the kitten home with her. On her front doorstep, she whispered, "It's time for you to meet your new big sister, Boo."

The kitten did not know what waited behind the big red door. *Hmmm*, she thought. *Who or what is a Boo?*

Jill turned the key in the latch—*creeeek*. The door opened, and there…sat…Boo! Boo was so very stunning. She was a glorious Norwegian forest cat with a luxurious long, full coat of gray, gold, and white. She had large, wise eyes that were a shimmering combination of yellow and green.

Boo was the kind of kitty who always seemed to know what someone was thinking about just by looking deeply into their eyes. She seemed like a queen to the little kitten as she sat there watching the newcomer. The kitten knew that Boo was a kind cat by the way she smiled: a small smile, but very sweet.

Jill gently set the kitten down as Boo, with a swish of her big, glorious, and furry tail, swung herself around and strolled away.

What did I do? Why is she leaving me? wondered the kitten.

At first, she sat very still, but she couldn't help stretching her neck and cocking her ears as she tried to figure it out. Getting curious, she started to walk slowly around the house, checking out every nook and cranny and sniffing here and there. Sniff, sniff, meow, meow. *Is it really true? Could this be my new home?* she wondered. All at once...she felt a whoosh of air and heard another swishing sound. It was Boo! The magnificent kitty of the house! She was back! Swoosh, swoosh! The kitten sat there quietly, waiting for Boo to speak. Boo said in a kind voice, "Hello, little kitten. Welcome to our home. I will be teaching you all the things you need to know in order for you to understand life in this great big world, and especially life here in your new home. Meow, meow, meow."

Boo talked slowly, and her cat voice and sounds were warm and soothing to the little newcomer. The little kitten started to purr, as she felt all warm and cozy inside.

"My name is Boo. Meow, meow," continued the magnificent furry cat. "I will be your big sister."

The kitten understood the *meows* of the cat language and could hear the kindness in Boo's voice (most humans don't take the time to really listen, but there are those who do and can understand the animal languages as well).

At that time, Jill walked in from the kitchen area, looked at the little kitten, and said, "It looks like you two are getting along quite well. I am so happy to be your new mama. When I first saw you, you looked just like a little lamb to me; a *little lost lamb.* But now you have a home and a mama and a big sister. You are part of our family, and you are no longer lost. I think I will call you *Lambkin,* if that is OK with you? This will be your forever home."

Lambkin thought about this. "Forever" sounded like *fur-ever. Fur-ever* was like the stuff that was all over her, lots of soft *fur* that made kitties who they were. This made her giggle.

With all of the excitement of the day, she was very hungry. She gobbled up the food and water that was already waiting for her. After that, Mama Jill gave her a nice warm bath. This made Lambkin very relaxed, and she loved the smell of the special kitty soap that Mama used. Mama Jill then dried her with a towel. By this time the kitten's eyes had started to feel sleepy. Her new mama picked her up and put her in a nice, soft, cozy kitty bed with the pink blanket and gave her a kiss on her little pink kitty nose.

Mama then gently picked up Boo and gave her a big hug and kiss, and put her in her own soft kitty bed.

That night Lambkin dreamed of all that she had seen and done during the day—the big outside world, wondering where she was, the chicken she had chased, her new home and family, and of course, her new name.

When the sunshine woke her the next morning, she realized that all she had dreamed about the night before was real, and most importantly, she had a family and a *fur-ever* home. Yawning a big yawn and then smiling to herself, she slowly walked out of her bed, one step at a time, as she was still quite sleepy.

Let's see what it is like being in my new home with my new family, she thought. Starting to get excited about what the new day would bring, she had an idea. "Maybe I will walk around and check things out like I did yesterday and even find more things to see and to play with. Why not give it a try?"

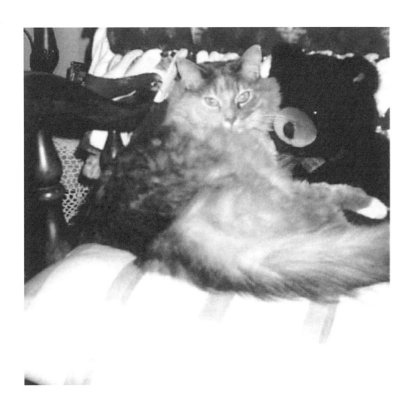

CHAPTER FIVE

A Bright New Day

It was a bright new day, and Lambkin was now a member of the family. A real family! And she now had a forever home. Gathering up her courage, she walked into the kitchen to find Boo already gobbling down her morning breakfast, along with Mama Jill, who greeted Lambkin with a comforting pat on the head. From then on, the day went by very fast. Boo had no problem sharing her toys with the new kitten, and the two of them happily rolled around on the carpet, playing with the many toys as they jumped, laughed, and had such kitty fun! There was always plenty to eat throughout the day, and after munching on treats that Mama Jill gave them, they were so happy that they ran around the whole house chasing each other and acting so silly.

At one point, Boo stopped the kitten and said, "So, little one, how do you like it here so far?"

Lambkin joyfully said, "I love it here. I love my new family, and I can't wait to meet some new friends! I love being silly and fuzzy!" Lambkin was in such a happy mood! She was feeling honored that she got to wear the collar with a little gold heart—it was just like Boo's, and Boo wore it so proudly.

There were still so many things to learn, friends to meet, and places to hear about. Lambkin wanted to be part of everything. That afternoon, when Mama Jill was baking cookies, Lambkin wanted to see what it was all about. When one of the cookies accidentally fell on the floor, Lambkin immediately jumped into action and snatched up a piece in her mouth. Mama did not like this, and took the piece of cookie right out of her mouth and said, "People food is not good for kitties, Lambkin. You will learn these things as you grow up."

Boo shook her furry head and said to Lambkin, "You must always listen to our mama, because she always knows best. Meow, meow… meeeeoooow."

Later that day, Boo sat down next to Lambkin and gave her some tips about this big world and how to deal with things. One of the things that Boo told her was that she was a very lucky little kitten. Not all animals in the world had it as easy as she did. Lambkin must always remember to be kind and polite to everyone, because she was one of the lucky ones. Boo explained that people are not always nice to the animals of the world, because they do not know how important animals are. She told Lambkin, "Remember to pass on to others all the things that you learn, and hopefully, one day, people will know that all creatures of this earth, big and small, are important, and that people need to treat them with much respect."

Lambkin shook her little fuzzy head and said that she would always remember to do this.

As Boo went off to lie on the windowsill where the sun was shining through, Lambkin perked up her ears and thought, *I have an idea. Why not give it a try? I will write a book! A great book!* And with that, she found a cozy spot right beneath the windowsill. She felt so peaceful and safe with Boo sleeping right there above her. Curling up and feeling ever so comfy, she fell asleep and dreamed of all of the things she would do someday. She dreamed about the great book she would write and how it would tell the whole world all about how important animals were and how it was so important to always be kind to them. She was a curious little kitty and she loved to learn as much as her little kitty head could hold. She planned to put everything that she learned into this book.

By this time, Mama Jill had come into the room where the two kitties were taking their afternoon naps.

What a lucky mama I am, thought Mama Jill. *I have two wonderful kitties that make me so happy*. And with that, Mama Jill covered them both with soft warm kitty blankets and kissed them both on their little soft fuzzy heads. *They will be up when they smell dinner later*, she thought, laughing.

CHAPTER 6

Tino the Mouse

The days went by, one after another, and all was fine in the house with Mama Jill, Boo, and the new kitten, Lambkin. Lambkin's fur colors started to change, and her new markings made her even more adorable. Boo and Lambkin got to be better and better friends, and they loved to play and spend time together. After all, they were now sisters. Boo continued to teach Lambkin, and Lambkin loved to watch Boo talk, as she looked so wise when she spoke of the many things that

Lambkin still needed to learn and understand. *Big sisters are so smart*, thought Lambkin.

One day as Mama Jill, Boo, and Lambkin were curled up on the couch watching a movie, when something ran across the floor. It looked like it was small, brown, and furry, just like kitties are. When Boo saw it, she muttered, "Oh my, I see *Tino* is back."

Mama Jill was already standing up by the time Tino got to the other side of the room. What a funny little creature he was—and a very curious one at that. Mama Jill looked down at Lambkin and said, "That is a mouse, Lambkin. A mouse is an animal even smaller than you are. No worries. I will make sure he gets back home safe and sound."

At that moment, Tino blurted out loudly, "Hi, Lambie!"

Boo had already known about this little guy for some time, as Tino the mouse had made a couple of visits to their home over the last few months. She had told Tino all about Lambkin. From then on, *Lambie* was her nickname.

Mama Jill opened the closet and pulled out a box from the top shelf. Inside was another box, which she put on the floor in the corner of the room.

"There," she said. "When he smells the food that I put in the back of this box, he will go into it, and then I can take him back home where he belongs. It is a special box that won't hurt him."

Lambkin was happy that Tino would not get hurt and that he, too, would get to go back to his home. *I love my home so much*, thought Lambkin. *I would not want to be away from my home either.*

Lambkin watched and waited for the next few days to see how this would all come together. Sure enough, one day Mama Jill found the mouse gobbling up the food she had put in the special box. After he was all done, she took the box outside and found an area in the grass where she could make sure he would be comfortable and able to find his way back to his own home. When she opened the box, Tino ran happily through the tall green grass on his way back to his little mouse home as he yelled out, "See you guys soon!"

That night Lambkin had another idea. She would help Mama with the chores the next day. *Mama works so hard*, she thought. *I will help her tomorrow. Why not give it a try? Mama will be so happy!*

With so many things to think about, Lambkin had trouble sleeping. Looking over, she saw that Boo was fast asleep already. *I am so lucky to have a big sister*, thought Lambkin. *I hope I can be as wise as she is one day, and maybe even as fuzzy and silly too!*

Still thinking about everything she had learned that day, Lambkin slowly drifted off to sleep. She dreamed wonderful kitty dreams about all the things that made her happy.

CHAPTER 7

Chore Time

How happy Lambkin was! She was sure that Mama Jill would be so glad to have her as a little helper with the chores. To get ready for the work, Lambkin did her exercises for the day, the ones that Boo had taught her. "This will make you stronger so that you can help Mama better," Boo had told her. "You will be strong like me in no time!" Lambkin even added some kitty yoga, which Boo had taught her one day when they both had some extra energy to use up. When they were through, Boo leaned over to Lambkin and said, "One day I will teach you how to dance. I think you will be a natural!"

Lambkin was not sure what dancing was and did not understand what Boo was talking about, but she was happy to have something to look forward to.

"Carry on, little sister," Boo said as she walked away to find a sunny windowsill to nap on. "Meow, meow, meow."

Lambkin was all ready to go as she saw Mama sorting out clothes. "Wheeee!" she said, jumping into the pile. "What fun! Meow! Meow!"

But it was work that Lambkin needed to help Mama with, and having fun could wait. Next, Mama Jill started to sort out some papers. Lambkin got involved right away. Finally, Mama Jill brought a mattress downstairs so that she could have it taken away. When the little kitty Lambkin saw the old mattress standing on its side in the living room, she immediately jumped on it and said to herself, *Mama needs me. I will take care of this silly old mattress.*

So she nipped at the mattress and made funny kitty noises as she used all her might to try to move it. "Please move!" she meowed at it. After all, Boo had told her that she was getting stronger from doing all her kitty exercises. "It should be easy for me to move this! Meow, meow! I am in charge here, mattress, and you must move!"

She continued to scold the mattress and scratch it for quite a while before Mama Jill walked in and said, "Lambkin! What are you doing, little kitty?"

Lambkin jumped to the floor. She had wanted so much to help her mama with the chores, and now she worried that Mama didn't see that. *Can't Mama see how strong I am and how I was making sure the mattress was listening to me?* she thought. She did not know that the mattress was not alive, and she had thought that she was showing it who was boss. She made a scrunchy kitty face because she was so confused. It was then that she noticed that Boo had been watching her the whole time. Boo leaned over to softly say, "Lambkin, you still have a lot to learn."

After the mattress was gone, a new one was put back in its place. When Mama Jill saw Lambkin and Boo talking, she went up to the little kitten and said, "You were such a big help to me today. I am so proud of you, sweet Lambie. Thank you so much! And Boo, you are such a good example for Lambkin."

The two kitties were so proud of themselves that they beamed with joy. With that, Boo leaned over and patted the little fuzzy kitty on the head with her soft paw. "I am glad that you are my little sister," said Boo. "I will always be here for you."

Lambkin felt so happy and so tired all at once. All she could manage to get out was a big "Meow!" Which was the most appropriate answer for such an event.

The Telephone

Mama Jill liked to talk on the telephone to her friends and family. Sometimes she would put the phone next to Boo, who would say some "meows." These "meows" were to other kitties on the other end of the phone. "Meow, meow, meow!" They had so much to say! Lambkin wondered what this was all about.

One evening when Mama was on the phone, she said, "Lambie, why don't you say something to my friend Deb's little kitty, Princess?"

With that, she held the phone up to Lambkin's mouth. Lambkin loved to talk, and sometimes she would even talk out loud to herself. She had a lot on her mind that day, and immediately blurted out, "Meow! Meeeeeooow! Meow! Hi, Princess. Will you be my buddy?" And then she said some other things, which went on for quite a while. Princess answered back with her own "Meow, meow," which seemed to be the right answer to Lambkin's question.

"Apparently, you had a lot to say to your new little friend," said Mama. "Always remember that you must be careful what you say to others. You must try to give good advice and help others when they have problems."

Lambkin said, "Okay, Mama, meow, meow."

Mama put a little stool next to her chair for Boo and Lambkin to sit on while they chatted kitty talk to Princess.

I love making new friends, thought Lambkin. Sometimes, she and Boo started meowing together, and it sounded a bit like they were singing their own special song. Other times, they talked over each other, and then Mama would say, "One at a time little ones."

"Meow, meow, meeooow," they said into the phone, while on the other end Princess meowed and kitty-chatted right back.

There were all kinds of other kitty noises that they made, and sometimes they got a bit loud with their meows and funny chirps. The kitties were pretty emotional about the things that they chatted about and they needed to vent their opinions on the topic of the day.

That night Lambkin thought of all of the cats that she still needed to talk to. She had heard Mama mention all of their names and was very anxious to have a chance to say some words to them when Mama Jill talked to their mothers.

There was Little Beans, Chaya, Mittens, Francis, Merlin, Magic, Jack, Mr. Owl, Trinket, Olive, Halo, Samantha, and so many others she had yet to chat with. She thought hard that night about what she would say, and she remembered that, whatever advice she gave, it should be good advice, and she would always try to help others with their problems.

"I must set a good example for all the other kitties the way that Boo does for me," she thought. "After all, Mama said I am a special kitty and that I need to make good choices. I will make Mama proud of me!"

CHAPTER 9

Ladybug Beetle

Ladybug Beetle was a clever little bug. She loved to play games with her bug friends, and she would often help them with their problems by talking and listening to them. By the time she met Lambkin, Lambkin had already heard about bugs from Boo. Boo had told her how tiny bugs were and that they needed to be respected too. All of the living beings on the planet should be respected and deserved kindness.

Boo told Lambkin that humans were the guardians of all of the living beings on earth and that bugs were often treated poorly because people did not like the way they looked on the outside. She also told Lambkin that Ladybug Beetle was a family friend who would come to visit from time to time. When Lambkin heard all of this, she was excited to meet this "bug," as she had seen such creatures but did not know much about them.

Boo introduced Lambkin to Ladybug Beetle when she came out of the corner of the living room to visit. Boo greeted Ladybug Beetle with a loud "Good Morning!" Although beetles speak a different language than kitties, it is all good, because when you care about someone, no matter what language they speak, you can pretty much understand what they are saying.

Ladybug Beetle had an elegance about her. She was so very beautiful and colorful. Lambkin thought that she must be a very special bug, and said, "Ladybug, you are so beautiful!"

Boo agreed and told Lambkin that Ladybug Beetle was indeed beautiful, but that beauty also came from the inside. Lambkin told herself that she would always remember this and put it in her great book.

Lambkin and Boo sat on the floor as Ladybug Beetle sat in front of them. "She is so tiny," Boo told Lambkin. "You must be very careful around her."

Ladybug Beetle talked about her day and told the kitties about the things she had seen outside of the house. Ladybug Beetle was gentle, and she made cute tiny bug sounds. She told Lambkin that she had found a tiny hole in the floor that she could crawl through to see the outside world once a day. She said that people did not understand bugs, but they were a part of Planet Earth too, and they meant no harm to anyone. After Ladybug was done talking, Lambkin began to understand what Boo meant when she said that beauty came from the inside. *What a kind little creature,* she thought. *When someone is kind and cares about others, then they are beautiful on the inside and outside. Being kind is such a warm and cozy feeling.*

CHAPTER 10

Helping Mama Feel Better

There came a day when Lambkin saw that Mama Jill was not acting the same. Lambkin could tell that her mama was not feeling well and wondered what was going on. She thought about this for a while before she decided to seek out Boo for some kitty wisdom. As she approached, Boo was relaxing and doing some kitty grooming, and was a bit groggy.

"What is it, little Lambie?" Boo murmured.

Lambkin blurted out that she was worried about Mama and did not know what to do. As Boo let out a big yawn—*Yaaaaawn*—she very slowly explained to Lambkin that sometimes humans get sick just like animals. "These things happen from time to time. Try not to worry, little kitten.

"It is always important to take care of your mama or whoever is your guardian," she continued. "Our mama takes care of us, and we need to take care of her too. Taking care of others when they need you is one of life's many lessons."

Yes…Boo was definitely wise, and looking into her beautiful yellow-green eyes always made Lambkin feel safe and warm and know that everything would be okay.

Still, Lambkin was worried about Mama Jill. She went on to eat her breakfast with Boo, which Mama had prepared. Lambkin made sure she ate every bite, as she knew that this would make Mama happy. Both Boo and Lambkin liked to see Mama Jill happy, as they loved her very much.

Next, Mama gave Boo and Lambkin special kitty vitamins that they ate every day. "My own mama taught me all about vitamins," Mama Jill said to the kitties. "It is very important to take care of your health, no matter how old you are. Always remember this, little ones."

Lambkin decided to never forget this. She had a lot of thoughts going around in her head, as both Boo and Mama had told her important things to remember. Lambkin even drank most of her water that day, thinking that this would for sure do the trick to make Mama happy. Hopeful, she watched as Mama did the dishes, but it still looked like Mama did not feel well.

Lambkin continued to ponder things for quite a while. Then she had an idea. "Why not give it a try?" Lambkin thought. "I know I can make Mama feel better. I will follow her around all day long, and by the end of the day, Mama will be all better! After all, I am so silly and fuzzy that Mama will feel better every time she looks at me. I will rub up against her and give her kitty kisses so that she knows how much I love her!"

Lambkin kept her word and followed Mama Jill around all day long, here, there, everywhere, into the kitchen and into the laundry room. She rolled on her back so that Mama could see how fuzzy her little tummy was. "How brave and magical I am," Lambkin thought. "I can make Mama feel better just by being around her!"

It was true. Mama Jill felt better by the end of the day. Lambkin knew it was because of her and that her love for Mama was the cure.

Boo eventually joined them, and the three enjoyed the evening together. Mama Jill truly did feel very loved and happy because her kitties were so caring.

That night, Lambkin curled up against her mama and placed her little paw in the palm of her mama's hand as she slept. Boo always slept next to Mama and was on the other side. She was already keeping Mama warm with her soft, full fur.

Lambkin started to yawn as she fell asleep. Loud purrs came from both Boo and Lambkin as they dreamed wonderful kitty dreams. "Purr, purr, purr."

Lambkin just knew that the three of them would always be together, forever and *fur*-ever.

CHAPTER 11

Baja the Pony

"Today is going to be a very exciting day!" thought Lambkin. "Mama says I get to meet Baja the Pony!"

Lambkin had heard about Baja the Pony through Boo. Baja lived next door. She was an Arabian pony with beautiful shimmering white hair and a blond mane. Days on end, she would peer over the fence to try to get a good look at the goings-on through the window of Lambkin, Boo, and Mama Jill's home. She would only get quick little glimpses of Lambkin and Boo rushing by the window when it was playtime. The times she liked best were when Boo slept on the windowsill and gathered up the sunlight. At these times, Baja stared at the kitty, wondering what life was like for a cat. Lambkin had yet to learn about the wonder of lying down on a windowsill and being able to see all that was outside of the house.

Later that day, Mama put a leash on Boo and put Lambkin in a pink kitty carrier. Boo called this box the *transporter* and explained to Lambkin that it transported kitties safely so that Mama could carry them where they needed to go. Lambkin liked the color and thought, "Why not give it a try?" Boo gave Lambkin a nod that all was OK, and from then on, the kitten was fine with being in the pretty pink box. The box even had an opening at the top where Mama Jill could pat the little furry one. Finally, it was time to go, and Boo excitedly started scratching at the door, ready to go on the adventure with the family. Today was the day they would go visit Baja.

Mama walked Boo on her leash and carried Lambkin in the pretty pink carrier over to the fence. The grass was especially green that day, as it had just been watered. It smelled so fresh and reminded Lambkin of the grass she played in at the Sunflower Drive-In. That day seemed so long ago.

Baja was enjoying the grass and had some in her mouth that she was munching on. Mother Nature seemed to have filled the air with happiness that day.

When Baja saw the group, she immediately trotted over to them. How beautiful she was! She had big beautiful brown eyes that gazed down on the little group. Her long eyelashes looked like feathers, and her eyes were so sweet that Lambkin instantly felt that Baja was a kind pony. Her white coat glistened in the sunshine. Lambkin became so excited that she burst out, "Meow! Meeeeeooowww!"

Boo was excited, too, and sat by the fence while she let out a couple of meows of her own.

"Neigh, neigh, neigh," Baja said back as she smiled a big pony smile and swished her golden-colored tail around. Swish, swish, swish.

Mama patted the pony on the head and said, "Hello, Baja. We came to see you and to wish you a great day. I hope you have been enjoying the beautiful sunshine." Next, she introduced the new member of the family. Lambkin stuck her little pink nose out of the pink *transporter* and gave Baja a big "Hi, Baja Pony!" Boo gave the pony a wave with her paw, and it was obvious to Lambkin that the two of them knew each other and were already friends.

Mama had brought a carrot for Baja to eat, and Baja gobbled it down quickly. For dessert, she had brought some sugar cubes. Baja started to prance around as she ate these up. The sun shined down on her in a way that made her seem very magical. Little pieces of light danced around her golden mane and looked like tiny sparkles. Baja was so happy that she did some more prancing. "Neigh, neigh, neigh." What a beautiful day it was for everyone!

I love meeting new friends, thought Lambkin.

Mama promised to visit Baja again soon and told her that she would bring her a nice big red apple next time they came. Baja then moved her head up and down as if to say, "Thank you. I would love that!"

What a wonderful day, thought Lambkin. *I met a pony and made a new friend all at once!*

CHAPTER 12

The Flower and Vegetable Garden

Boo and Lambkin both loved to watch Mama work in her garden. They could see her tending to the garden through the glass door. Sometimes Mama would leave the glass door open but keep the screen door closed. This way, they could feel the breeze coming through, and they could smell all of the garden smells. They just loved the smell of the fragrant flowers. There were all kinds: petunias, roses, daisies, and many more. The lavender was one of Mama Jill's favorites. Mama Jill picked flowers from the garden every week to put in her cherished purple vase. She also had some vegetables growing in the garden and would often share these with friends. Sometimes the smells made Lambkin sneeze and make a scrunchy face. The garden had little statues all around, and both Boo and Lambkin loved to try to pose like the statues. This would make Mama Jill laugh. It really was a sight to behold, as it was very adorable.

One day, when Mama was busy at work in the garden, the two kitties were laying side by side, passing the time and watching every little thing she did. Lambkin saw that the screen door was open a bit. A mischievous idea popped into her little fuzzy head. *Why not give it a try?* she thought.

With that, she squeezed her fuzzy little kitten body through the opening. "Just a little bit more and I will be outside!" She took just a few more steps…and there she was, standing right in the middle of the flower, herb, and vegetable garden!

"This is beautiful!" exclaimed Lambkin. "And it is even prettier than when I see it through the screen door!" The whole garden seemed to surround her with color and smells. There were green colors, pink colors, purple colors, yellow colors, and orange colors. And so many shapes! A couple of little red balls with pointed tips were sticking out of the ground right next to her. *Hmmmm*, she thought, taking a little nibble out of one of them. *What is this? Maybe I will take another bite.* Then suddenly, "Blahh!" It was bitter and tasted terrible! "Yuck!"

She had taken a bite out of a red radish, and now she had a horrible taste in her mouth! Trying to spit it out, she made a funny sound. By that time, Mama Jill had noticed her. "How did you get out here so fast, Lambie? What are you doing?"

Lambkin did not know what to think of the red balls. *Why did they taste so bad? What are they?* she thought.

Boo sat quietly and watched from beyond the screen door. "You silly little kitty" she said. "Meooow, meooow!"

Mama Jill scooped Lambkin up in her arms and took her inside. "Radishes are not for kitties, little one. They are people food. You need to drink some water to get rid of that bad taste in your mouth. And here, eat some of your kibble too."

Lambkin was already slurping up the water. It dripped all over her mouth and fur and on the floor as she hurriedly drank and drank. Suddenly, she started to hiccup. "Hic...Hic...Hic! What is going on with me? Oh, dear! Hic, Hic, Hic."

Finally, after she had drunk most of the water in her kitty bowl, she stopped making the hic-cup noises. "I will never eat those red balls ever again!" she said to Boo. "Meow, meow, meow!"

By this time, Boo was shaking her head and saying, "Oh my, you are so silly! First the cookie and now this. What a silly little kitty you are! You learned another lesson today, little sister. Be very careful what you eat, and don't ever eat something if you don't know what it is."

Lambkin felt a bit foolish, but she was glad that the taste was gone from her mouth. "Meow, meow! What an adventure!" she exclaimed. "What next?"

CHAPTER 13

Girls' Day

"Oh, what fun!" blurted out Lambkin. "It is Girl's Day!"

Mama Jill had taken out most of her jewelry and was organizing it on her bed, while Lambkin and Boo peered around the corner, curious to see what this was all about. Lambkin could not take her eyes off the pieces of sparkly jewelry. *This is beautiful!* she thought. The sparkles of the jewelry reminded her of the sparkles of sunlight she saw around the gorgeous pony Baja.

Lambkin and Boo both got involved and happily walked around the jewelry to make sure nothing had fallen on the floor. They both felt that they were helping Mama by doing this.

Lambkin did not know it, but Boo had always loved jewelry. Boo loved sparkly things so much! When she was just a kitten, she would secretly take pieces of jewelry that Mama Jill had left in the bathroom on a tray. She would pick them up in her mouth one by one and drop them behind the bed so that she could play with them later. Luckily, they were too big to swallow. Eventually, Mama found the jewelry and just laughed and laughed and didn't seem to mind at all. She just said, "I see you like jewelry too, little one. I guess it is a girl thing!"

When Boo saw all the jewelry on the bed, she remembered how she used to hide it behind Mama's bed and how Mama had said it was a "girl thing."

Lambkin started to prance on the bed, as this was something she had seen Baja do. *I can prance too, just like Baja!* she thought. *What fun this is!* She saw a twinkle in Boo's eyes and could tell that Boo also loved playing with all of the shiny and sparkly jewelry. So much fun! Little sparkles were everywhere!

This does not seem like work at all! thought Lambkin. Boo and Lambkin continued to examine the pieces of jewelry, to make sure they were OK and ready for Mama Jill to work with. Boo called it "jewelry inspecting." When they were done, Mama Jill carefully put all of the little sparkly pieces of jewelry into plastic bags so that they would be safe, but she left out a couple of pieces for the kitties to play with. This made Lambkin and Boo happy as they scurried around, playing games with the pieces. They pushed the pieces around on the floor with their little kitty noses and then jumped on them. Then they ran around and around the room, shouting, "Meow! Meow!"

Mama Jill knew that this meant they were enjoying themselves and having kitty fun.

Later that day, Lambkin and Boo took a nap while Mama Jill painted her toenails. They cuddled up next to her, and she was careful not to wake them up. They looked so soft and sweet, purring as they slept. The sound of sweet purrs is so calming and Lambkin and Boo loved to make this sound.

"Purr, purr, purr."

I am so lucky to have such sweet kitties, Mama Jill thought.

When the two kitties finally started to wake up, they yawned and looked at Mama as if to say, "What is next?"

The three of them realized that it was getting time to eat dinner. Mama Jill put all of the jewelry away and said, "Time for dinner, sweet kitties." And with that, the two kitties were wide awake. All three of them hurried down the stairs to eat. The kitties were so very hungry. After all, they'd put a lot of energy into helping Mama. Work can be fun too! "I love it here!" Lambkin exclaimed.

"Me too!" said Boo. "Meow! Meow! Meow!"

The two kitties meowed so much that Mama Jill had to laugh. "You are both so silly," she said.

After dinner, both kitties started to purr again: "Purr, purr, purr." All was good in their home tonight, and it was time to get some rest so that they could be fresh to start the next day with more fun and adventure to come.

"Time to get cozy," Lambkin said as she scurried back up the stairs with Boo close behind her.

CHAPTER 14

Books, Books and More Books

Days went by, and Lambkin learned that there were many, many books in the house. They were over there...and there...and on top of there. She often climbed on top of them pretending that she was very, very tall. Mama Jill loved to read and had many bookcases of books in her house. It seemed like she had a library in the house, and she often lent books to friends who also liked to read.

"Maybe I should learn to read," Lambkin thought. "I love it when Mama reads to us, but maybe I can read something to Mama."

One day, Lambkin thought she would give it a try. "Why not?" she thought. So she jumped onto one of the bookcases and looked for some-thing to read.

I like the colors on this book, she thought. *Look how big it is. The colors remind me of the pretty colored flowers in Mama's garden. I will give this one a try.*

With her little kitty paw, she pushed the book, and then pushed it again, and suddenly it fell to the ground along with several other books that came toppling off of the shelf! "Whoops," she said. "I think I made a mess. Meow, meow, meow! Uh-oh."

The pages of one book fell open. *OK then,* thought Lambkin. *This is the one I will read.*

She tried to read the words, but being a kitty, she did not always understand what they meant. Luckily, Boo had come into the room and saw what Lambkin was doing. Boo was very proud of the words she knew and loved teaching them to Lambkin. "Those books look awfully big for a little kitty to handle. Just work on the words I have already taught you. I will teach you everything that you need to know, just like I always have. Be patient, little kitten. You have done well, and you seem to have remembered many of the things that I passed on to you during your lessons."

Lambkin was listening to her big sister, but she was also looking at the pictures that were in the book. "Look at this picture!" she burst out.

"Yes, there are many pictures of animals in that book," said Boo. "Animals that you have not heard about yet. I know you will carry on the message that all animals are important.

Hopefully, one day all humans will realize this and will respect all the creatures of the earth."

Someday, I will be able to read anything! Lambkin thought in her little kitty head. *After all, I am a very smart little kitty.*

At this time, Mama walked into the room. "What are you two up to?" she said. "I bet you would like me to read you a story. What do you say, little ones?" She picked up the book that Lambkin was looking at, sat down, and began to read a story about animals that were far, far away. Lambkin relaxed, as she liked the sound of her mama's voice. When Lambkin heard Mama read the word "food" in one of the sentences, she got excited, because it was a word she was very familiar with. Immediately, she perked up.

"Is dinner ready?" she said. "Meow, meow?"

Boo had already fallen asleep as Mama continued to read.

When Mama Jill got up to make dinner, Lambkin had fallen asleep too. She was dreaming once again, of the great book that she would write and of all the things she would talk about in it.

Mama said, "Okay, little ones. When you wake up from your kitty naps, your *food* will be ready for you."

With this, Lambkin perked her little head up yet again. "Did someone say *food*?" she asked. "Meow?"

Then, once again, she dozed off.

Letting out a chuckle, Mama thought, *I love my sweet kitties so much, and I love our little family.*

CHAPTER 15

Still So Much
to Learn

Lambkin, Boo, and Mama Jill all loved to sit next to one another and be cozy on days when there was no work to do. Mama continued to read books out loud for the kitties to hear. Although Lambkin and Boo did not always understand what Mama Jill was reading, they did understand that Mama was happy. Her voice made them calm, and they knew that this was a happy time. There were also many more words that Boo understood, and Lambkin was starting to catch on to these too. Also, just by watching their mama they could learn about many different emotions.

Days went by, and there were many happy occasions for the little family to celebrate. Birthdays and holidays were always full of fun, and they always had a wonderful time. One day in the springtime, the sun was especially warm, and Lambkin decided to "Give it a try" and follow Boo's example of lying down on a sun-filled windowsill. There were three windowsills altogether that Lambkin had discovered. She had seen Boo lie on all of them at one time or another, but she had always lain on the floor beneath the windowsill in the past. Now she decided to venture forward and be like Boo. "Time to give this a try." She slowly walked up onto one of the windowsills, and she realized that she could see so many things outside that she had never seen before. *Is this how Boo learned so much about the outside world?* she wondered. *Wow! Everything is so pretty!*

There were flowers that were all different colors like the ones in Mama's garden, as well as bushes and trees that were very, very tall and had pointy tops. She had seen some of these things when she was a little lost kitten, and she started to remember how alone she had felt at that time. Looking back outside, she saw that the trees looked like they were almost touching the sky! There were so many things to look at. Suddenly, it occurred to her that she might be able to help Mama by guarding the house while looking out this window. She felt so proud that she had thought of this, and she decided that she would make it her job.

Every day, she made sure that she looked out the front window to see if anything was out of order. She felt just like a detective! She had seen a picture of a detective called "Nancy Drew" in a book that Mama had read to the kitties.

As she continued to watch day after day, she saw the most amazing things. She saw little winged creatures flying through the air, which Mama called *birds*.

I remember seeing these too when I was outside and all alone, she thought. She saw what Boo had told her were *dogs*. They were on leashes similar to Boo's leash. People walked around with the dogs, and the dogs seemed to love to roll around in the grass, barking and just having doggie fun. "Ruff, ruff!" went the dogs. "Ruff, ruff, ruff!" Every once in a while, Lambkin yelled out loud, "I want a puppy dog! I want a puppy, Mama!"

One day, there were children playing outside. One of the children was pushing the other children around and being a bully. Lambkin was not sure what this was all about, but she knew that it was wrong. Immediately she began to scratch at the window and yell out loud. "Meow! Meow! Meeooowww!" Which meant, "Stop that! You need to be kind to each other. Boo told me so!"

She got so upset that Mama Jill rushed over to her and said, "What is wrong, Lambkin? Are you OK?"

Lambkin let out a very long "Meeeoowww!"

Startled, Mama looked out the window and saw what was going on. She left the house and found the mother of the child who was doing the bullying. They had a nice talk, and from that time on, Lambkin saw that the children were always kind to each other and played nice. "This is amazing!" Lambkin thought. "Being kind is really as important, as Boo told me it was."

Lambkin was so proud of herself and thought that this was something she would write about in the great book she was planning to write one day.

What a lucky little kitten I am, thought Lambkin. *I am so very fuzzy and silly, and now I am becoming so very smart. I have learned so much already, and I can't wait to learn even more! Meow, meow! I love my fur-ever home and my family so much. I can't wait to have some more adventures!*

HERE ARE SOME OF LAMBKIN'S FAVORITE THINGS TO SAY

Why not give it a try?

That is so silly.

Is it time to eat yet, Mama?

That is funny, Mama.

What is going on, Mama?

Where is Boo?

I am such a fuzzy and silly little kitty.

Time to get cozy.

Work is fun.

Oh, the silliness of it all!

Please play "The Puppy Song," Mama.

I am a sleepy little kitty.

HERE ARE SOME OF LAMBKIN'S FAVORITE THINGS TO DO

- One of Lambkin's very favorite songs is "The Puppy Song" by Mr. David Cassidy. Lambkin loves to run around when she hears it, and I truly think that she is trying to say that she wants a puppy too. Lambkin says, "Check out his song on YouTube and run around like me!"
- Another song that Lambkin likes is "In My Tree" by Mr. Kyle Vincent. She says that it makes her really think about other animals and how important they are. Check it out.
- Lambkin loves eating kitty treats, and Mama Jill makes sure they are the healthiest ones.
- Lambkin loves to sleep in soft cozy blankets.

- Lambkin loves to run around the house with Boo as fast as she can go and then jump into piles of tissue paper.
- Just like Boo, Lambkin loves to sleep in the sunshiny rays.
- Lambkin loves to giggle with Boo for no reason at all.
- Lambkin loves to hear stories about other animals.
- Lambkin loves to be a detective.
- Lambkin loves to do kitty yoga.
- Lambkin loves to be silly and fuzzy.
- Lambkin loves all animals big and small.

Lambkin Word Search

```
B T V W V L J T Y T R M A M A P Y
E T K H W Y A L W A H A P P Y S Z
A N Y I L L L M L I E S M B R J T
U W Z S N I M L B V D S L A T S V
T T J K S B O Q O K D M E E W T J
I O T E Q C R L L N I X A A E R Q
F Y W R Y Y R U E D L N P N Q P R
U S V S D P F I L A M B I E N Y N
L X L D Y Y R E G G N U J W F K Y
R D V Z A F B X Y W Y R S F M Q N
M G Z L K L R R N E Y J U I V Y R
Y U P J I V B P U D S L K R C P B
F M Z Z T N T Y P S F Z P T A I L
X M R K T N O B B B H J U W X Y N
Y T Z Y Y D N S P J O K R J D B D
M L Q L P V N R E T P O R R Q R J
```

Beautiful
Boo
Brush
Collar
Ears
Eyes
Fluffy
Friends
Fuzzy
Happy
Kitty
Lambie
Lambkin

Love
Mama
Music
Nose
Paws
Playful
Purr
Silly
Sleep
Tail
Toys
Whiskers
Widmann

153

Lambkin Word Search Key

CPSIA information can be obtained
at www.ICGtesting.com
Printed in the USA
LVRC081138140521
686679LV00047B/566